PASTOR'S STUDY

KABINETT

—— & ——

KAMMER

SEAN SCHERER'S
KABINETT

SEAN SCHERER | FOREWORD BY **ANDERSON COOPER** | PHOTOGRAPHS BY **WILLIAM ABRANOWICZ**

DRAWINGS.

& KAMMER

CREATING AUTHENTIC INTERIORS

VENDOME
NEW YORK · LONDON

Contents

Foreword

I first read about Sean Scherer in the *New York Times*. It was a big article about Kabinett & Kammer, his antiques store in the Catskills. It must have been around 2009. I had bought an old firehouse in Greenwich Village and had spent months restoring it and making it into a home. There are a few converted firehouses in Manhattan, but most of them have been stripped of their identity. My partner and I didn't want to do that.

The building was from 1906 and we loved its history. We wanted to restore it and honor all the people who had worked in the firehouse over the decades. We also wanted it to be an expression of our varied interests and travels. We talked about making the firehouse into a kind of cabinet of curiosities. We wanted it to be like the home of an explorer from the turn of the century, a personal museum full of the art and books and objects we'd both collected over the years.

I wasn't looking for an interior designer, but I loved the pictures of Sean's store I saw in that article, so one weekend we drove upstate to visit his shop. As soon as we got there, I knew this wasn't going to be just a quick browse and a single purchase. There was such thought put into every object—its placement, its patina, its relationship to other objects nearby. There was nothing precious about Sean's taste. Some of

---

Opposite: Vintage sporting photos and gym equipment add period-appropriate charm to a room in Anderson Cooper's converted firehouse.

Overleaf: A school chart of the anatomy of a frog is a surprise guest in the kitchen.

9

"SEAN HELPED US CREATE A HOME
THAT SPOKE TO THE HISTORY
OF THE BUILDING—AND OUR OWN
PERSONAL HISTORIES."

———

the things he had on display were beautifully polished or in great condition, but many of them weren't; they had scratches or scuff marks, paint was cracked or peeling off, but that made the objects more beautiful, more unique. You could see their history, you could feel it, you could tell how they had been held and used. This was not a store where you couldn't touch the antiques; these were objects that called out to be picked up and examined.

That first visit, we ended up buying a large, framed anatomical chart, likely once used in a classroom sometime in the early 1900s. We told Sean about what we were hoping to do with the firehouse, and he generously took us to look at his home in nearby Walton. As you will see in the pages of this book, the rooms in Sean's home are filled with a remarkable mix of color and texture, and surprising pairings of objects that make you stop and smile. Sean's interiors are sophisticated and well designed, but they feel completely natural, as though they have just evolved over time. He has a unique ability to place otherwise ordinary objects in a completely unexpected context or grouping, and in so doing change the way you see them.

Visiting Sean's house, I knew he could help me create the home I had always imagined. I asked him to help us with the firehouse, and before we knew it, he was sending us pictures of amazing finds: an enormous chest of drawers from an old factory; well-worn, antique carpets; a merchant's counter from an old shop in upstate New York that became the centerpiece of our kitchen. Sean helped us create a home that was a complete reflection of our varied interests and tastes, a home that spoke to the history of the building—and our own personal histories.

In this book Sean Scherer shows us all how to create unique sanctuaries for ourselves, without spending ridiculous sums of money. These are rooms within reach. Imaginative spaces that are authentic and honest, designed to be lived in and loved.

Enjoy!

Introduction

The art director Paul Rand once wrote,

The artist is a collector of things imaginary or real. He accumulates things with the same enthusiasm that a little boy stuffs his pockets. The scrap heap and the museum are embraced with equal curiosity. He takes snapshots, makes notes, and records impressions on tablecloths or newspapers, on backs of envelopes or matchbooks. Why one thing and not another is part of the mystery, but he is omnivorous.

Rand's observation has always resonated with me. Growing up in Miami in the 1970s and '80s, I avidly absorbed the strange milieu of my hometown, collecting bits and artifacts of my environment like a field scientist or a scavenger. The Miami of my youth was a world of incredible contrasts. There was both glittering history and urban decay, wild natural beauty and human-made political unrest. My birthplace itself exemplified these striking contrasts. I was born in Mercy Hospital, built on the former manicured grounds of Vizcaya, an elaborate early twentieth-century re-creation of a Venetian villa on Biscayne Bay. The hospital's brutalist main tower building still peers through the overgrowth that was once part of Vizcaya's 180 acres of gardens, architectural follies, and lagoons built out of the native mangrove hammocks.

Opposite: On this 1853 map of Florida, Miami appears as little more than swamps and wilderness.

M-281 VILLA VISCAYA, MIAMI, FLORIDA

Left: A 1960s postcard of Villa Vizcaya, showing its vast original gardens.

Below: Vizcaya's iconic stone barge also acts as a breakwater in front of the original main entrance to the villa.

Opposite: In Vizcaya's ornate enclosed loggia, authentic European antiques mix with trompe-l'oeil painting and eighteenth-century-style scenes that may have once been stage sets.

One of America's premier Gilded Age mansions, Vizcaya was the winter residence of James Deering, a son of the founder of Deering Harvester Company, which eventually became International Harvester. Grade-school field trips introduced me to Vizcaya. It was also where I had my first showing as a very young artist—at the age of fourteen—in a weekend art festival.

In collaboration with designer Paul Chalfin, Deering created one of the most authentic and human-scale masterpieces of the era. In comparison to Vizcaya's sensitivity to scale, Vanderbilt's Biltmore seems more like an overblown Hollywood set out of an Orson Welles film. Vizcaya doesn't try to impress you with its volume. And its multi-layered interiors seduce you into submission. Today, one might call the merging of elements from different periods and styles—with the emphasis on creating a mood or experience—eclecticism, as opposed to an attempt to design a historically faithful reproduction.

With the help of his team of artisans, Chalfin fashioned three-dimensional assemblages that feel original and lived in, as if these rooms had been inhabited for generations. They were theatrical, to be sure, but I was used to theatrics, thanks to our annual family trips to Walt Disney World and my immersion in the work of Miami architect Morris Lapidus. When I was a youth, I believed that Vizcaya's rooms were genuine historical representations, with wall coverings, art, furnishings, and objects all shipped over from Europe, and I fell utterly for them. Only later, after years of education and experience, did I see Chalfin's magic.

Time, or more precisely the passage of time, is essential to an authentic interior; it must feel as though it has organically and gracefully progressed through the years and generations. I always try to create the sense that a space has naturally evolved, adding furniture or pieces that are not perfect, or just a little off. Chalfin understood that, sometimes seeking out objects with noticeable damage or repairs. A real home would never be perfect!

Opposite: The reception room at Vizcaya is lined with custom-made palm-tree wallpaper.

Right: A CAUTION sign at Fairchild Tropical Botanic Garden warns visitors to beware of crocodiles.

In retrospect, it was this odd accumulation of different influences, moods, and textures that laid the groundwork for my magpie sensibility. Like a little boy stuffing his pockets, I soaked it all up and have carried it with me throughout my life as a painter, a collector, a designer, and a general hobbyist of all things beautiful.

For a kid growing up in Miami, the world was full of beautiful adventures. We visited Fairchild Tropical Botanic Garden and picnicked under the moss-laden live oak trees. We ran around ponds encircled with danger signs warning of crocodiles. We swung from vines and howled like Tarzan from colossal banyan trees in Merrie Christmas Park. We cycled through the mangroves to Parrot Jungle and Matheson Hammock Park. How many kids learn to swim in a Venetian-style, 800,000-gallon freshwater

swimming pool converted out of an abandoned coral rock quarry, replete with waterfalls and caves? Anything seemed possible, and very little seemed unimaginable.

Vibrant color was everywhere—every possible variation and combination of greens, and blues ranging from the clear skies to the blue-black storm clouds to the aqua of the shallow shore and the cerulean of the deep ocean. The sun seemed to shine endlessly. And besides all that, there was the incredible visual jolt of the gray cast-concrete architecture set against the brightly hued flora and fauna of the subtropics. So my sense of vivid color and contrast was ingrained at a very young age.

The politics, however, were a very different story. Miami was then in the early days of its transition to becoming the unofficial capital of Latin America. The Mariel boatlift

Above and right: In the Miami Beach of my youth, the signature Art Deco architecture was mostly whitewashed and decaying.

Opposite: Golfers on the Biltmore Hotel's course in 1939, when the hotel was in its prime.

in 1980 had brought an estimated 125,000 Cuban refugees to Florida. I came of age when there were bumper stickers with sayings like, "Will the last American leaving Miami please bring the flag?" Miami, known as The City Beautiful, was now "Paradise Lost," according to an infamous November 1981 article in *Time* magazine. This beautiful place had become a center of violence and drugs, as fictionalized in Brian De Palma's film *Scarface*. It was a turbulent era, a combustible mix of beauty and anger.

The young city had already seen its share of boom and bust cycles. I was growing up during one of those busts, a time of decay and abandonment. The Biltmore Hotel, for example, loomed large over the suburb of Coral Gables, an ungraceful shadow of its former self. In its heyday, it had been one of the most fashionable resorts in the entire country, hosting royalty of both the European and Hollywood variety. The Duke and Duchess of Windsor, Ginger Rogers, Judy Garland, and Bing Crosby had been frequent guests. Everyone from politicians like President Franklin D. Roosevelt to notorious gangsters like Al Capone stayed at the Biltmore. They enjoyed fashion shows, gala balls, aquatic shows in the 23,000-square-foot grand pool, elaborate weddings, and world-class golf tournaments.

But in 1942, the War Department took over the hotel and converted it into a 1,200-bed military hospital. Its windows were sealed with concrete and its travertine floors

Retirees soak up the sun in 1970s South Beach, as documented by photographer Andy Sweet.

were covered with layers of government-issue linoleum. It remained a hospital (and served as the early home of the University of Miami's School of Medicine) until 1968. Thereafter, it sat abandoned and boarded up for the next twenty years, a giant gray ghost hovering over the banyan tree–lined streets and golf courses of Coral Gables.

Like the Biltmore, the Art Deco district in Miami Beach suffered a steep decline. Most of the more than 800 Art Deco hotels and other structures built between 1923 and 1943 in the heart of the district, now known as South Beach, had become decrepit, and many were abandoned. The area was impoverished and rife with crime. No one cool ever went there. The oceanfront hotels were turned into makeshift retirement homes for mostly Jewish residents. They would sit on their aluminum and webbed-plastic folding lawn chairs on the once chic terraces. For me, these buildings were relics of a bygone era: highly aestheticized, streamlined concrete structures fading and cracking in the baking Florida sun, inhabited by elderly folks who seemed equally forgotten. A palpable, melancholic sense of loss hung low in the air. But to me, it was also a very romanticized one as well. I guess that is why I have always been attracted to the forgotten or less than perfect, so growing up in Miami at this time was perfect.

People are always surprised to find out that I was born and raised in Miami; in fact, the most common response is, "I didn't know anyone came from there." In the history of the world, Miami is an infant, the invention of developers who lured northerners down south with fantasy residential developments built out of the coral rock foundation of the city. So how did a kid growing up in a twentieth-century environment that had been nothing more than swampland at the beginning of the 1900s learn to love antiques? Perhaps it is because I grew up in Miami at a time of loss and decay and romantic ruin, exploring amid the wreckage of old monuments like the Biltmore, that I love the discarded, the unwanted, and unappreciated.

Another important fact about my childhood is that I never lived in the same house for more than a few years. My parents were into DIY way ahead of their time. They also had the house bug and spent most weekends driving around, with my two siblings and me in tow, visiting open houses. With my mother's interest in interior design and my father's hobby of home renovation, the duo of Art & Diane could not be stopped. We were always on to the next home-renovation project. Because it was the only way of life I knew, it seemed perfectly reasonable, and besides, it was exciting and fun. I was able to see firsthand and at a very young age the potential for physical transformation and the power of creating transformative spaces. The first time I heard that a friend had lived in one house for his entire childhood, I thought how odd that was.

One of my earliest recollections is of being placed in a fold-down child seat on the back of my mom's bike. The iron seat was painted black and had a thin, blue-and-black-plaid cushion. I think the bike was blue too. I remember the seat being very uncomfortable, with the metal supports pressing through the flimsy foam cushion, and it certainly had no shock absorbers. Since my mom did not drive, this was our form of transportation. We would go all over Coral Gables together: the usual trips to the big Publix supermarket, with its winged Art Deco architecture, and then off to the Cocoplum Women's Thrift Store and the nearby secondhand-clothing store.

Housed in a grand old Spanish Colonial–style building, the thrift store was my favorite place. Once I was in my seat, we would pedal over the concrete canal bridges and around the traffic circles until we arrived. Mom would secure a spot along the coral rock wall and lift me out, and we would pass through the towering, dark brown wood doors and enter this wonderland of discovery. Rows and rows of boxes filled with unknown treasures, furniture such as dressers, tables, chairs, and credenzas pushed up against the walls. It was overwhelming, but so exciting. I loved those damp, overflowing cardboard boxes. I still feel the same thrill and get butterflies in my stomach when approaching an antiques fair or yard sale—anticipating the moment when I spot that unique object, the one that calls my name to rescue it, take it home, and give it pride of place.

As I grew older, we would venture farther afield with my mother's best friends, Ginny and Sharon, who drove. We would go to the antiques shops housed in warehouses in Homestead and to Cauley Square. It was on one of the trips to Homestead

that I made my first official purchase with my own money. I was sixteen. It was a brass Art Deco clock. It didn't work when I bought it, and it still doesn't, but the fact that it was a clock was secondary. I was fascinated by its shape and outline, the possibility of its future, and the mystery of its past. That first purchase began my love affair with objects and the stories they tell, or more appropriately, the stories and memories with which we endow each one of our finds.

Being the youngest, with five and seven years separating me from my sister and brother, respectively, I was left to my own devices. I would spend hours outdoors, climbing trees and catching lizards, but I spent even more time indoors, creating. I would build imaginary sets out of wooden blocks and Legos, adding anything else I could find. I remember making a whole miniature amusement park out of thread and my mother's pink plastic hair curlers in the empty bottom space of my trundle bed. I worked on it for days. There was a Ferris wheel, a skyway like the one I had ridden many times at Walt Disney World, and countless other dreamed-up attractions, each of which I rigged with guide wires out of sewing thread to make the parts move. Like a carnival barker, I summoned the neighborhood kids to behold my miniature spectacle. I'm not sure they saw the fantastical creation as I did, but they always seemed amused and entertained, which made me happy.

I was always drawing, whether architectural floor plans or imaginary housing developments filled with glass brick–wall details. Everything was painted pink and aqua. The house designs were almost always Art Deco and Bauhaus inspired. With these first imaginary house plans, I began to practice my skills as a designer, learning the importance of shape and form, balance, and spatial concepts.

My main influences were the whitewashed Art Deco buildings of South Beach, the high-rises by the up-and-coming architecture firm Arquitectonica that were beginning to sprout up along Brickell Avenue, and the great Morris Lapidus resort hotels like the Fontainebleau and the Eden Roc. What a fantastic place to grow up, amid wire

Opposite and below:
Arquitectonica's primary-colored buildings, including the Atlantis condominium with its five-story palm court and red spiral stair, were an inspiration to me.

Right: Fantasy over function: Morris Lapidus's famous stairs to nowhere in the Fontainebleau Hotel.

staircases in hotel lobbies that led nowhere and buildings with giant squares cut out of the centers that might feature a cadmium-red spiral staircase and a palm tree too.

My dad was an airline pilot and was away a lot on extended trips, so my mom was often left alone with us. Because she didn't drive in a car-oriented city like Miami, she devoted much of her free time to indulging in amateur interior design. She would often rearrange our living room furniture, swap pieces out for new vintage finds, and paint surfaces over and over. Some objects would acquire a thick skin from the many layers of color changes. There were always stacks of interior design magazines piled up in the house, and I would spend hours flipping through them on rainy days.

Two of her books fascinated me. One was *Converted into Houses* (1976). It featured all sorts of industrial spaces, from warehouse lofts to tugboats and even an icehouse, that were made into homes. Loft living was entering the mainstream, and I couldn't get enough of it. I looked at the book over and over, always finding some new detail. What I gleaned from it would come into play many years later when I wound up living in an old factory loft on Duane Street in the heart of Tribeca. The other book was an extra-large copy of Audubon's *Birds of America*. My mother always displayed it open, on a 1970s metal faux-bamboo console table. It felt enormous to me then. I would sit crossed legged, with the larger-than-life book resting in my small lap, and pore over every gloriously illustrated page; when I came across a double-page spread, it was all-engulfing. It's funny how all these early seeds were planted, how so many influences were laid out before me. The colors and all those exotic birds swept me away. At such a young age, my passions for design and natural history were cemented.

After graduating from high school, I left Miami to attend the School of the Art Institute of Chicago. The year was 1986, and Chicago was not yet the cosmopolitan metropolis it is now. It was a culture shock for a kid who had grown up in Miami to discover such a different part of America. Don't get me wrong; there is much fantastic art and architecture in Chicago, but it was so gray and the winters were bitter cold. I went from a subtropical, multicolored hothouse to a cold, steely gray Midwestern city that was like nothing I had ever experienced before. I felt transported to another planet. Where were the abundant sun and inexpensive seafood? And where did that palette of green, blue, and aqua go? It was stark and

PLATE CCCXXI.

Roseate Spoonbill.
PLATALEA AJAJA. L.
Male Adult.

Engraved, Printed and Coloured by R. Havell, 1836.

As a boy, I pored over my mother's extra-large copy of
Audubon's *Birds of America*. Roseate Spoonbills were a
common sighting on childhood field trips to the Everglades.

severe in comparison to my hometown. Yes, the Wrigley Building and the architecture of Louis Sullivan and Ludwig Mies van der Rohe were inspiring, but nothing as light and airy as that of the Art Deco district. Even the heaviness of the coral houses in the Gables seemed to float like Macy's Thanksgiving Day Parade balloons next to Chicago's architecture.

During the holiday and summer breaks, I would return to Florida, but my family had moved a bit north to Tallahassee. With me behind the wheel, my mom and I would continue our antique and vintage buying trips. Towns like Havana and Quincy in northern Florida and Quitman and Thomasville in southern Georgia provided a treasure trove for us to pick through. The antiques and vintage stores then were filled with one-of-a-kind primitive pieces. They were often painted in pale greens verging on teal or more than occasionally in grassy green, colors that harked back to my Miami roots. I favored simple, angular shapes with no fancy details or extras—boxy shapes that reminded me of Bauhaus architecture or the streamlined Art Deco hotels of South Beach.

Thus, my early love of architecture was reflected in the furniture forms I began to acquire. One of my first pieces, which I still have, is a grain-painted box with a downward-sloping, two-door lift-top front on round feet. It's very structural, almost house-like, but what drew me to it was that this heavy volume was raised up on four perfectly carved round feet, lightening the whole. It also has a faint reddish-orange hue that seems to be coming from within instead of just being applied to the surface. Another early piece, and probably my favorite, is a five-tiered, rounded crockery bench or plant stand. It is one of my few concessions to the curve, but it is also very vertical; it stands tall on flat boards with cut-out half rounds for feet. The construction is pure and simple. It's one of those useful objects that I adore. Painted in that grassy green, it reminds me of the giant sweeping arc of Lapidus's Fontainebleau.

While at the Art Institute, I began to paint more seriously and decided to focus my attention on becoming a painter. Neo-Expressionism was all the rage then, but I was drawn to early Modernism and, more precisely, to the Russian Constructivists. All the exposure to the architecture of Miami had left its mark. Despite Chicago's renown for exemplary architecture, from Sullivan's early skyscrapers to Mies van der Rohe's International School masterpieces, I never felt at home. I stayed only a few semesters before applying to the Whitney Museum of American Art's Independent Study program in New York. After I was accepted, I moved to the Big Apple, which was the obvious place for me. In choosing to go to Chicago first, I was trying to avoid the inevitable, and it did help provide a transition to the big city.

At nineteen years old, I was the youngest person in the program. The studios were at 384 Broadway, in the area south of Canal Street known as Tribeca. We had weekly

This green-painted plant stand, a favorite early find, now displays a
collection of cell models. The sailboat artwork is by Tracy Holman,
and the silhouette of Rocco, my dog, is by Carter Kustera.

An untitled 1990 painting is an example of the
exaggerated patina and use of geometric patterning
that was characteristic of my early work.

reading seminars and visiting-artist lectures. I had a fantastic year living and working in downtown Manhattan. I remember my first trip to SoHo, getting off the subway at the Spring Street station at the corner of Spring and Sixth Avenue, and the feeling of exhilaration that came over me. It was alive and still funky then. Frame shops abounded, and the artist-run FOOD restaurant was hip. The original Dean & DeLuca was there, overcrowded in its small space. It felt like a small town in the big city.

I met the artist Ross Bleckner at the Whitney program. He was the first person to buy one of my paintings. And I exhibited at the Artists Space gallery, in its selections show. One day during the show, a man approached me and expressed interest in buying a painting. He was friendly and ended up buying two. When I asked for his name and address, he wrote down Edward Albee, so my second collector was one of the most esteemed American playwrights, author of *Who's Afraid of Virginia Woolf?* Tribeca was like that then. It wasn't very populated, and you would run into the same people on the street every weekend. I started showing in numerous galleries and had quite a bit of success. My first solo show, at Stux Gallery on Spring Street, sold out, and there was a time when there was even a waiting list for my paintings.

The concept for my paintings then was not far from my interest in the old or forgotten during my formative years in Miami. I would age my pictures with stains or watermarks, creating the sense of the passage of time, of well-worn but beloved objects. I also often painted on a ground of asphaltum, similar to roofing tar thinned with mineral spirits. That pitch-black tar ground created an unstable painting surface, as the asphaltum would soak up the top layers of oil paintstick. Some critics likened it to stonewashed denim and dismissed it as purely nostalgic. But for me, it was always about the impermanence of things.

While I was working in New York as an artist in the late '80s, the 26th Street flea market was as defining to me as the Limelight was to the club kids I would occasionally run with. One of my finds, purchased from a grizzled dealer displaying his wares on a shabby card table, was a nineteenth-century English Staffordshire tureen. The shape, reminiscent of a Rococo folly, was the opposite of modern. It had the traditional transferware landscape in red and white, bordered by an ornamental pattern called Gothic Beauties. A friend pointed out that the old soup bowl I had just wasted my money on would look ridiculous on the black mid-century coffee table in my white Tribeca loft. And besides, "Why does a twenty-one-year-old kid want a tureen anyway?" But I had spent years riding around on the back of my mom's bike, going to thrift stores, and she taught me something about instinct. It seemed like a good deal, and as it turned out, I was right. While I was pursuing a career as a painter, my love for old objects and the forgotten and unfashionable continued unabated.

In the 1990s I moved to Paris and was immediately taken with the city, especially its massive flea market, Les Puces de Saint-Ouen, the street florists' amazingly simple bundled bouquets, and the incredible antiques stores of Le Marais. These curated shops contained some of the most beautiful objects I'd ever seen. They were old-school antiques dealers with individual voices expressed in small, jewel-like boxes hidden behind ordinary storefronts. Walking into each one was like entering a full-scale Joseph Cornell box. The art and objects displayed in these shops had real history, the kind of magical tales found in items that bear the human imperfections of the handmade. And that is what I love to use as my medium, objects whose story is still evident. In addition to frequenting the flea markets and antiques stores, I would spend hours in the Louvre and other museums. I often took the train on weekends to other cities, including Colmar, Basel, Cologne, and Vienna. One Easter weekend, I visited all the châteaux of the Loire Valley. It was there where I understood Chalfin's brilliance in his creation of Vizcaya. Paris was the best education a young artist could ask for.

After Paris, I had stints in Buffalo and Toronto before returning to New York City in September 2000. I found a place in the Seaport area of lower Manhattan, determined to revive my stalled art career, but I had been absent for too long, and the market had also changed. My place in it had slipped away. I spent a year struggling to find my grounding and was not sure of my next steps. I sold a work here and there and did some other jobs to support myself.

On a Tuesday morning in September 2001, I awoke, opened my shutters, and immediately spotted a large group of people on the street corner below. They were all looking skyward; following their gaze, I saw a massive trail of white papers flying through the air. It was the beginning of days and weeks of traumatic experiences.

Living through the recovery and constant reconstruction was taking its toll. At this time, my best friend, Deborah, invited me to come upstate to get a break from all the chaos. She had recently purchased a small farmhouse with a barn in the Catskills. All I knew about the Catskills came from movies like *Dirty Dancing*. I had never been to that part of New York before, but it took only one morning, waking up to birdsong and the magnificent mountain view, to get hooked. With my art career stalled and not much else keeping me in the city, I decided to make a permanent move upstate.

I found an 1840s Cape-style farmhouse and set about renovating it. I couldn't imagine making art at this time, so my house became my artwork. It was also a way for me to restore my senses, to rebuild my soul and faith in humanity. I soon found a community of like-minded artists and designers. My little spot in Delaware County was quickly feeling like home. I also began teaching design and art history at SUNY Oneonta, and soon after that opened my store, Kabinett & Kammer.

The storefront of Kabinett & Kammer in Franklin, New York.

THE
Odd Shop

I opened Kabinett & Kammer in 2007 at the urging of my friend Brooke Alderson. The name comes from the German words for "cabinet" and "chamber." At the time, Brooke owned Brooke's Variety in the town of Andes, New York. An actor famed for roles such as John Travolta's aunt in *Urban Cowboy*, Brooke's personality is larger than life, and that carried over into her shop. With walls painted in bright Mexican hues and funky painted furniture, the place was brimming with odds and ends and had become a Catskills destination.

Opposite: A cadmium-yellow wall provides a colorful plane to offset the water buffalo mount and surrounding objects.

"STYLES COME AND GO.

GOOD DESIGN IS A LANGUAGE, NOT A STYLE."

——— MASSIMO VIGNELLI ———

It was at a dinner party at my house that Brooke prodded me to consider taking my home to the people. I had been scouring antiques shows and flea markets for decades, but oddly, the thought of opening a store had never crossed my mind. There happened to be an old corner store with floor-to-ceiling windows available; it had been the town's original post office. It seemed like the perfect spot to give it a try.

From the outset, I strove to create a store that would feel at home in Miami or Paris, New York or London. With what I had learned from Brooke, I wasn't going to dumb down the aesthetic or try to make it feel more country oriented. The whole store would be a revolving work of art and would act as a laboratory for my evolving collections and displays. I also wanted to emphasize the modernity of the utilitarian pieces I favored: objects and furniture that people had made in their barns for specific purposes and uses. They weren't intended to be artistic, but simplicity combined with practicality—plus years of use—had transformed them from the ordinary into the extraordinary. I would build narratives around these objects, linking different items by color or shape but also juxtaposing them in surprising ways. It was all about the story and sharing my knowledge. To my surprise, the shop became an instant success.

———

Opposite: In the shop window, dramatic light casts old paintbrushes, an Italian tole sconce, and a pair of Audubon prints in sharp relief.

Overleaf: The Odd Shop sign, one of my favorite early finds, has been a fixture in Kabinett & Kammer and welcomes visitors with a clear announcement of what's in store.

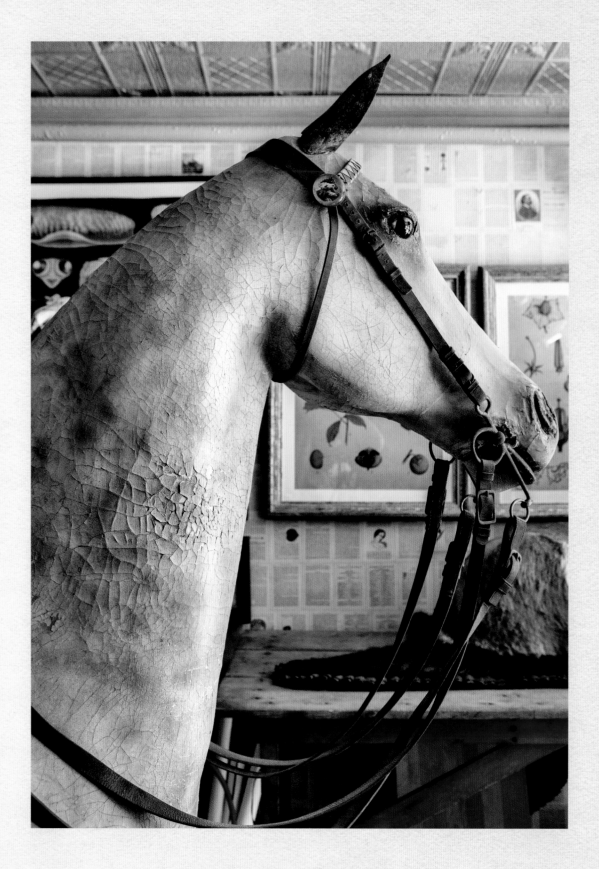

Above: A life-size papier-mâché horse, originally part
of a saddle display, stands proudly in the center of the shop.

Opposite: An old anatomical chart of a shark is a perfect
example of raising the ordinary to the extraordinary.

Opposite and above: A decaying general store in upstate New York creates an excellent environment for
an eclectic array of art and objects such as an antique anatomical model, paintings by Luke Dougherty,
and a photograph by Saxton Freymann below a full deer mount and a caribou rack.

Above: Stacks of tin and wood boxes can make a
significant decorative statement on a tabletop or shelf.

Opposite: Have fun incorporating found objects such as
an old scale and clock face into your décor.

Above: Enlarged photos of vintage trays become ornate and surreal wallpaper—
my homage to Vizcaya. Brass candlesticks hold handmade candles by Greentree Home.

Opposite: I always imagine the shop experience as the equivalent of
walking into a life-sized Joseph Cornell assemblage.

Opposite: Mustard, circles, and reds! The recurring circular motifs keep your eye flowing in and out. The reds of the cabinet, rope tapers, and flour sifter connect this array of disparate finds.

Right: Patina perfection. This playful grouping of painted tin and metal candleholders is an excellent example of masculine and feminine forms working together.

———————

Overleaf left: Flags make historical and incredibly colorful backdrops.

Overleaf right: Red, white, blue, and pink. Intense colors make good company. The brightly painted cabinet couldn't be more cheerful and is the perfect companion for the Italian tole rose branch. The graphic bicycle poster picks up the red and pink, continuing the sunny theme.

No.4
Building 410

Geometric educational charts and an enlargement of an eye with its parts labeled hang over a well-worn workbench in the shop and serve as inexpensive contemporary art.

51

Opposite: An ornithological collection, formerly in a university, flocks together in an oak display cabinet.

Above: A single specimen stands out against a wall papered in old book pages.

———

Overleaf: Warm red-browns and rustic wood textures create great silhouettes in the whitewashed shop.

RHUBARB

AQUA
FOENICULI

FERR.
ALBUMINAT.
SOL.

Opposite: A large apothecary cabinet from a
local hardware store fills an entire wall in the shop.

Above: Once a staple of nineteenth-century homes,
old invalid feeders peek out of many of the cabinet's drawers.

LIGHT
REFLECTIONS

Mirror, mirror on the wall, who has the fairest collection of them all?
Why Kabinett & Kammer, of course! There is always a vast assortment of antique and vintage mirrors in my shop; they are one of my mainstays. I have a passion for them, the old wavy-glass ones especially, but all mirrors from the 1850s to the 1950s are fair game to be thrown into the mix.

There is barely a room in this book without one. Why is that?
- Mirrors reflect, and what they reflect can add light and volume to a room.
- They make a statement and have a presence in any interior.
- Mirrors make easy art and are readily available too.
- They come in many styles, from small, square, unadorned shaving types to ornate carved-and-gilded sculptural follies.
- A cleverly placed one can lead your eye into an adjacent room and expand the scale of a small space.

To give them a more significant impact, one technique is to group them.
Combining straight-edged, curve-topped, and oval ones is always a good idea. A grouping of smaller mirrors instead of a single large one creates a more sculptural effect; each mirror refracts the light differently, accentuating the three-dimensional display. Mixing in deeply layered antique frames and other objects adds to the fun. In the picture on the facing page, the mirrored effect carries through to the tabletop, where a scalloped vanity mirror, a mercury-glass lamp, and a collection of mercury-glass vases playfully multiply the reflections and light. The final touch is the dark gray-blue wall, which sets off this beautiful vignette and intensifies the reflected light.

Who's Afraid of Red, Yellow and Blue?

The title of this chapter comes from a series of paintings by Barnett Newman, who was referencing Edward Albee's play *Who's Afraid of Virginia Woolf?* Newman's paintings are in primary colors and pack a visual wallop. So many of us seem to be scared of using color, real color, in our homes. The default is usually white or off-white. But that is a shame. Your body responds to the color of a room in the same way as it does to temperature and light. Just think of the tropics. Using true colors—cadmium yellow, cobalt blue, forest green—rather than washed-out pastels, can lift your spirits. We all have a favorite color. If you work off that, you can create a whole room that elevates your soul.

Opposite: Vintage school models of the lungs sit atop a wonderfully crackled, red-painted sideboard that I picked up on a buying trip in the Deep South. A homemade black-and-white officials box makes great Op Art and ties in with the abstract lung sculptures.

And you don't have to limit that color to the walls. A customer once came into the shop and chose a bright yellow tin box. As she placed it on the counter, she explained that she was going to build a whole color story around this one box and change up her living room.

It is natural that way, using small items to add hits of bright color. And you can carry the same color around a room, just as an artist uses similar colors in different parts of a painting to keep your eye moving. They can even flow subtly from room to room to help transition. So go ahead, be bold!

———

Above: Dishes and juice glasses add bursts of color to open shelves.

Opposite: A fresh coat of maroon paint makes a big statement in this compact kitchen.

Preceding pages: A bold color choice can make passageways as impactful
as the grandest of rooms. In a dimly lit area of the landing, an array of mirrors reflects
light from the window opposite and creates volume.

Opposite: Even sparse accent colors, like the yellow pillows, green candles, and green-
painted chairs, can have a significant effect in an otherwise crisp white dining room.

Above: A bright yellow wall projects the art and a mid-century Scandinavian
ceramics collection into the room in almost a 3-D way. The pulley illustrations in the
mechanical chart are echoed in the shapes of the winged ceramics.

Preceding pages: Wash away your troubles with a leisurely soak in this
inviting bathroom. A small seating area and floral-patterned rugs over well-
worn floorboards lend it the look of an old English country cottage.

———

Opposite: This bedroom is a study in masculine geometry and bold color. Navy-blue walls and
a crazy quilt found on eBay envelop the sleigh bed in a cozy cocoon of pattern and warmth.

Above: A red-and-white-striped painting of mine and a watercolor
by Roxy Paine dominate a corner of the room.

———

Overleaf: Sleeping nooks are a staple of my home renovations. Based on Old World
European box beds or cupboard beds, which were designed to maximize space and retain
warmth on cold winter nights, now they just entice you to take an afternoon nap.

Pages 74–75: The palette of this bathroom derives from the faux Van Gogh haystack painting picked up in a local vintage shop. Basing a color scheme on a favorite object is a beautiful way to infuse a room with your personality. A guest bedroom opposite the bathroom continues the theme.

Preceding pages: Custom wallpaper, created from enlargements of photographs of the early blue transferware dishes in the cabinet, covers an entire wall in this living room. The blue is picked up in the denim sofa and two toile-patterned throw pillows.

Pages 76–77: Tucked behind a door, this corner of a living room gets a rococo treatment. The playful arrangement draws your eye to the corner, while the mirrors connect it to the rest of the room, drawing your eye back out.

Above: A detail of the collection of early Staffordshire transferware dishes.

Opposite: Taxidermy and natural objects create a sculptural effect.

CARAMBOLAGES
OLD HOME LOVE
A BEAUTIFUL MESS
THE WAY WE LIVE
Alpine Interiors
Country Interiors
London Interiors
Paris Interiors
AXEL VERVOORDT
BOHEMIANS
Perfect English Farmhouse
HANDCRAFTED MODERN

Above: Aquamarine walls enliven the entryway of a nineteenth-century Cape house.

Opposite: Even though there are a lot of different objects in the entryway, arranging them symmetrically creates balance and calm.

Preceding pages: I love using intense colors in small spaces such as this landing and hallway to liven them up. Farrow & Ball's Arsenic was an almost exact match to the original paint color uncovered during the renovation.

Opposite: A low-ceilinged stairwell and landing are wrapped wall-to-wall in a toile de Jouy wallpaper to expand the limited space. It's another design trick to make the most of what you have and to animate an otherwise dull space.

Right: In this kitchen, bright blue walls, a vintage botanical chart, and a yellow mod fiberglass chair are all it takes to pack a graphic punch.

Overleaf: Two staircases, one in a large formal home and another in a cottage, demonstrate the significant impact that bold color has on spaces often thought of as mere pass-throughs.

Pages 90–91: Cheerful colors help homeowners stay upbeat on cold winter nights. Aqua walls combine with naturals like raw linen and primitive wood furniture, as well as with vintage kilim pillows and rugs, to cozy up this living room.

"COLOR IS A POWER THAT
DIRECTLY INFLUENCES THE SOUL."
—— WASSILY KANDINSKY ——

LIVE
COLORFULLY

Red, yellow, blue, aqua, mustard, and teal, to name but a few bold interior color choices. Color is everywhere in nature, from the vermilion of the royal poinciana tree to the brilliant blue of the hyacinth macaw, but when we shut our doors to the outside world, we often shut out living with color too. Why is that? Why be afraid of color? Most of our living spaces come as blank canvases, usually covered in a flat-white contractor paint, ready for a more individual and authentic hue—that flat white is crying out for your personal touch. However, a lot of us wind up living with white walls that would be better suited for a doctor's waiting room, cold and impersonal.

- Small objects and decorative items such as pillows, flowers, candles, painted boxes, linens, and vases can also have a huge impact. They are an easy way to bring color into your home and can also be changed with the seasons.
- You can build off a favorite color or color range; in the interior on the facing page, I worked with a palette of yellows and greens. Yellow is woven throughout, connecting disparate objects, including the acid-yellow Murano glass vases, the sunflower-yellow metal tea cart, the arrangement of daffodils, and the lemons in the tole wall sculpture. There are even dabs of chrome-yellow oil paint on the artist's palette. All these yellow touches keep your eye moving like a pinball bouncing off bumpers. The greens ground the exuberant yellows and give the interior a tropical Miami vibe. The green wall, botanical prints, tapers, painted boxes, old painted cupboard, and staghorn fern bring your eye back down.
- It is all about the play and compositional balance.

This Is Not — a Pipe

Artists like Marcel Duchamp and René Magritte understood the power of taking ordinary objects and putting them in unexpected contexts. It frees them to be appreciated on their own merits and enjoyed in a whole new light. The same concept applies to the most exciting and playful interiors. It's all about creating a surprise scenario and storyline. Almost any object can benefit from this approach. Anatomical models created expressly for teaching purposes can appear as abstract art when removed from the classroom setting. A brightly painted shoeshine stand with an oversized footrest mounted on a wall instantly becomes a sculpture, delighting the eye and surprising the mind.

***

Opposite: A taxidermy swan hovers above a painted country cupboard with an abstract art–like patina. The openwork structure of an Asian root table and a scholar's rock adds to the organic mélange and counterbalances the cabinet's hard edges. The shape of the scholar's rock echoes the arched shape formed by the swan's wing. An abstract painting by Deborah Schneider makes it all seem contemporary.

It can be as simple as hanging an antique carpet on the wall. What's usually under-foot is now a work of art, just by changing the perspective. It can also highlight an object's geometry and patterns. Mashing up eras is another fantastic way to break objects free of their past. A nineteenth-century painted cupboard might go all but unnoticed when surrounded by the usual period suspects. But put it in a clean white setting, and suddenly its distinctive lines shine. To me, period anything is a bore. Mix things up, break norms, and have fun. It's your home, after all, and should be the place that represents you the most authentically.

Above: Play with combining objects of similar shape
to create dynamic still lifes. Imagine them having a
conversation about how they relate to each other.

Opposite: Three or more of the same object can constitute a
collection: fire extinguishers, tin boxes, old file boxes, and pails
are all lifted out of the ordinary when seen in multiples.

In a converted firehouse, the ground floor has been transformed into a kitchen. A few large pieces, including an antique store counter that serves as an island and a tall file cabinet, add scale and counterbalance the ornate spiral stair.

"LOOK AT
USUAL THINGS
WITH
UNUSUAL EYES."

———

VICO MAGISTRETTI

Opposite: A collection of heart models is surprisingly juxtaposed with an Andres Serrano photograph and a perfectly preserved column from an old house porch.

Right: Lend a hand: a shelf bracket displays a stand-alone anatomical model.

101

Above: Modern and primitive mix effortlessly in a simple but
powerful arrangement consisting of three elements.

Opposite: In a kitchen pantry, the open shelves of a corner cupboard provide easy
access to the antique ironstone serving dishes, which are on display when not in use.

―――――

Overleaf: Art and taxidermy fill a hall from floor to ceiling,
creating an immersive museum experience.

Left: We often register visual resonances unconsciously, even subtle ones like the sidearm curve of the grand piano and the bend in the elbow of the prone figure on the first-aid chart.

Opposite: The silhouette of the Noguchi lamp mimics the figure on the blood-vessel chart.

Overleaf: Antique French paper targets hang over a mantel decorated with ironstone tureens. The handles of the dishes' covers both echo and point to the bull's-eyes in the art above.

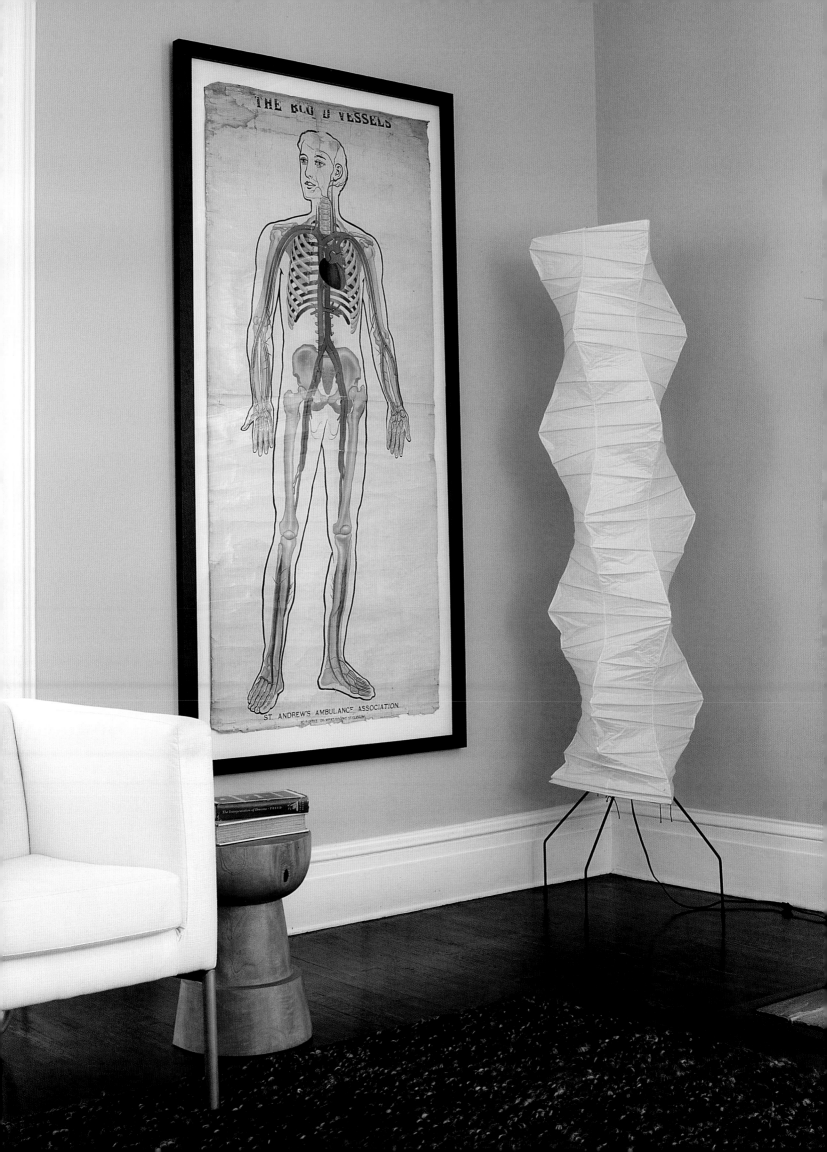

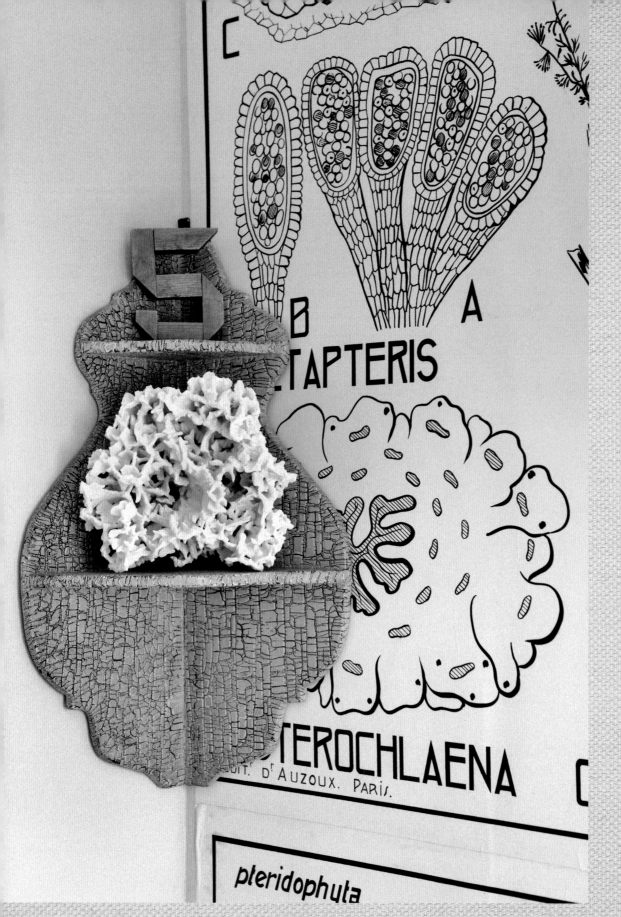

TAPTERIS

B   A

TEROCHLAENA

DIT. D? AUZOUX. PARIS.

pteridophyta

Preceding pages left: A doctor's model of a foot is a surprisingly cheeky addition to the ironstone covered dishes and the torso print.

Preceding pages right: A first-aid chart illustrating different head bandages fits in perfectly among the newel posts and turned-wood balusters of these stairs.

Left: Picking up motifs and repeating them in three dimensions, a crackled corner shelf mimics the cell structure in the wall illustration, as does the coral.

Opposite: Going big in a small space: covering the walls of this small room with enlarged prints of old school charts makes it feel more expansive. Limiting the palette to black, white, and neutrals adds a sense calm and allows for more textural additions. The black and white of the wallpaper, zebra stripes, and cowhide rug unifies these varied elements visually.

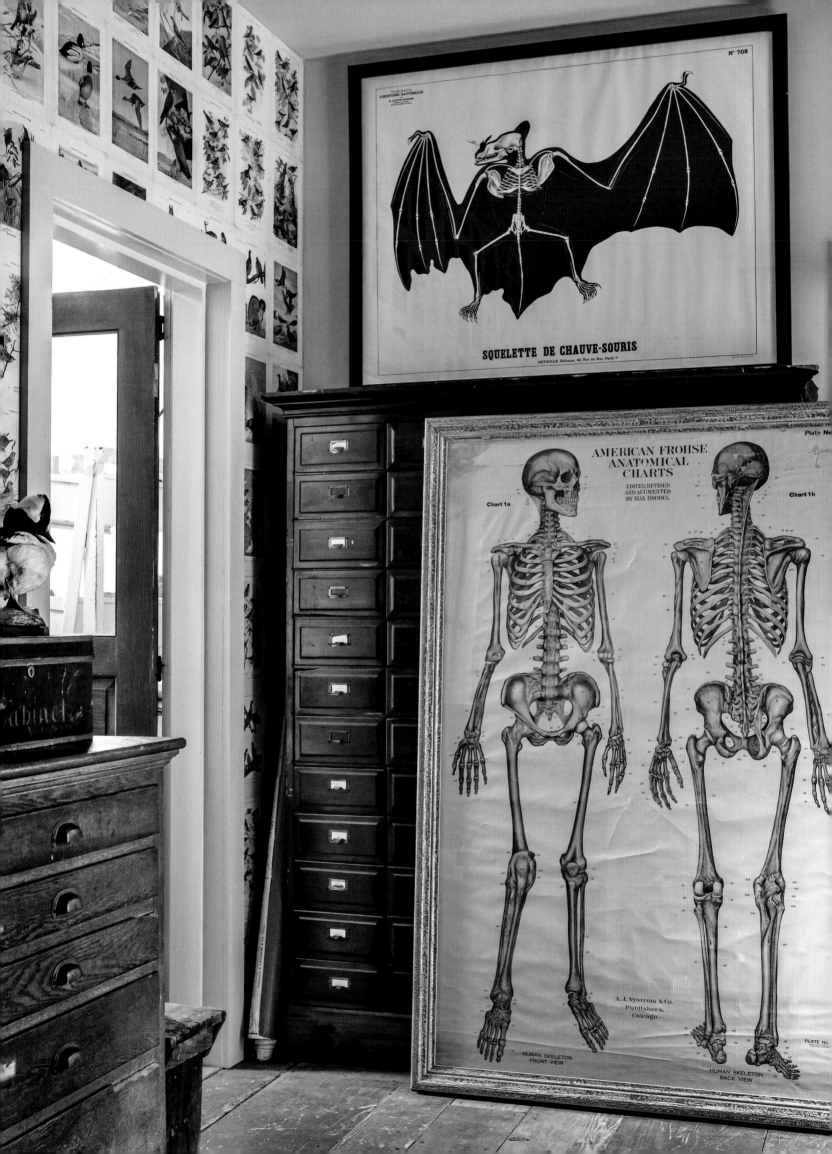

SQUELETTE DE CHAUVE-SOURIS

TABLEAUX
D'HISTOIRE NATURELLE

N° 708

DEYROLLE, Éditeurs, 46, Rue du Bac, Paris 7e

AMERICAN FROHSE
ANATOMICAL
CHARTS

EDITED, REVISED
AND AUGMENTED
BY MAX BRÖDEL

Chart 1a

Chart 1b

Plate No

A. J. Nystrom & Co.
Publishers,
Chicago

HUMAN SKELETON
FRONT VIEW

HUMAN SKELETON
BACK VIEW

PLATE NO.

Preceding pages: A lot is going on in this dining room with a natural-history-
museum vibe, but because the colors are limited to grays, whites, and browns,
it has a somewhat minimalist quality and does not overwhelm.

———

Opposite: A storage room filled with filing and flat-file cabinets houses numerous prints.

Above: Pages from *Birds of New York*, a book that was a gift from a friend,
create a lighthearted wall covering.

Opposite: Seek out unique objects to create personal narratives.
An old plaster rope–adorned shelf mixes effortlessly with a pair of paint-
encrusted architectural brackets and a vintage carved bird.

Above: A mid-century gilt sunburst mirror is a rococo folly in an otherwise
rather masculine room. It is always a good idea to add a bit of whimsy!

Above and opposite: Two wholly different vignettes
share an orange and blue color combo.

SURPRISE
AND AMAZE!

Change the meaning of an object by changing how it is usually seen.
We are used to seeing objects in their familiar environments, but when we free them of that, we let them be reborn. A deer mount that is perfectly at home in a traditional cabin or a hammerhead shark commonly seen floating above restaurant-goers in a seafood shack become surprising sculptural art when placed in a contemporary setting. Mixing a number of such objects on one wall or in a single room, as seen on the facing page, creates a surrealistic effect. It is a time-honored trick of many artists and easy to apply to any living space. Old educational charts and prints, with their bold graphics and scientific diagrams, are another example. Once framed and separated from their classroom setting, they become instant avant-garde artworks.

With this approach, anything is fair game . . .

· Everyday objects can rise to the level of art. Architectural fragments, vintage machine parts, rusty farm tools, and old advertising signs can wow when seen in a new light.

· Seek out objects of striking color, texture, and silhouette. When displayed en masse on a wall or mounted on a stand, they will pack a visual punch.

· Another way to change the perception of objects is to pair them with objects of a different era. Think a nineteenth-century painted cupboard with mid-twentieth-century ceramics on top. It's the jarring juxtaposition that provides the joy.

More
— Is —
Less

Forget about the minimalist dictate "Less is more." "More is less!" I believe. There has always been power in numbers. However, there's a difference between mere clutter and objects that make up a collection. Minimalist artists understood this. Multiples of an object add meaning to even the most mundane of household items. The smallest things can be become grand in scale when displayed en masse. There is a prevailing aesthetic that espouses empty plastered walls with few artifacts or furnishings, but that look is tough to pull off without appearing pretentious and cold. The trick is to contain and control what might otherwise devolve into clutter. Be maximal without becoming overwhelmed.

Opposite: An 1853 map of North America sets the tone for this tabletop arrangement. Sixties-era brass lamps with vintage fiberglass shades are a marriage made in heaven. Bunches of grocery-store flowers are a great way to add color and bring in the changing seasons.

One way to maintain control is to use symmetry. Balance adds calm. Starting with a central focus point and building outward gives the illusion that there are fewer objects. It also allows for variation within that symmetry. Another tried-and-true method is displaying a whole collection in a small confine such as a traditional cupboard or a shelf niche. The natural boundaries of the space will keep it all in check. Salon-style hangings, which have been around since the seventeenth century, are a great way to display many pictures in a limited amount of space. Hanging pictures from floor to ceiling instead of in the usual single eye-level row creates a stunningly visual dynamic. But because there is more art than empty wall space, your eye merges the pictures into an overall pattern. So it doesn't feel busy at all.

With a few of these time-tested tricks, you can not only have and display all your favorite artifacts but also turn your interior into an art installation.

————

Above and opposite: The graphics on a graduated set of Art Nouveau pitchers riff subtly on the Chinese Art Deco rug and aqua round table. Neutrals ground the room and allow for hits of color in the upholstery.

Preceding pages: A two-car garage has been transformed into a salon filled with an assortment of cabinets that house collections. The cement floor has a faux-stone painted finish.

Right: A mantel is topped by a collection of cell-division models, and a glass-fronted cabinet with a pink interior displays groupings of rock specimens. Painting cabinet interiors is another smart way of adding hints of color to a room.

1918 SEPTE

SUN.	MON.	TUE.	WE
1	2	3	4
8	9	10	1
15	16	17	1
22	23	24	2
29	30		

"EVERY OBJECT TELLS A STORY IF YOU KNOW HOW TO READ IT."

── HENRY FORD ──

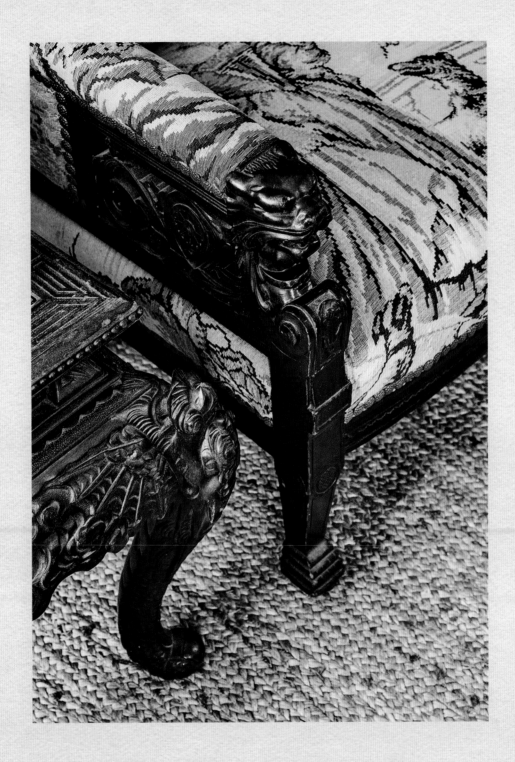

Preceding pages and opposite: A windowed interior wall allows light to pour from one room into another. It's a trick dating back to old nineteenth-century buildings. Think banks with their glass-walled offices.

Above: An intricately carved wood side table and a tapestry-covered chair pair well with rush matting.

Opposite: Corners often go unused but are excellent spots to display
a collection, adding interest in an otherwise blank space.

Above: A symmetrical arrangement and the repeat of round convex mirrors ringed with balls—as is the
fireplace fender beneath them—create a balanced, triangular composition that your eye follows.

Overleaf: A custom-built curved bench fits this cozy corner of a taproom and
provides maximum seating. The choice of blue is a fun surprise.

Preceding pages: An architectural fragment from a fireplace surround
has been repurposed as a bar back. Mirrors help reflect the light and
create the illusion that the shallow bar is deeper than it is.

———

Opposite: A gallery-style wall in a café elicits memories of old country diners.

Above: A vintage Salami on Rye sign from a New York
deli becomes instant and wry kitchen art.

Preceding pages: A wall of glass-fronted storage cabinets is pressed into service as a pantry. Seeing the contents not only facilitates organization and retrieval but also is a visual pleasure.

Opposite and above: Textured earth tones in fabrics, rush matting, and a faux-wood-grain-painted chest richly layer this room. A pink taxidermy flamingo cuts a slender figure against a vintage Belgian tapestry and ups the fantasy ante.

Preceding pages and above: A beach cottage is decorated with an array of small mirrors and antique prints. The crab specimen anchors the display with joyful aplomb and welcomes in the summertime fun.

Opposite: Plaster-and-wood palm fronds from an old Miami Beach motel get a creative new life as a fireplace screen.

Overleaf: Mantel tops naturally invite a revolving assortment of your favorite objects and collections. Usually the focal point of a room, these stages are just waiting to be set. One of the beloved items on this mantel is a small whale watercolor by Mary Maguire.

Opposite: A collection of steamship prints hung gallery-
style keeps this seaside guest bedroom on theme.

Above: A playful vignette of ceramic mushrooms and a
taxidermy duck greets guests in the morning.

Overleaf: Filling the walls of a small bedroom with large-scale
framed prints makes it appear more expansive.

Opposite and above: It's all in the layering: patterns on top of patterns, wallpaper, curtains, carpets, and upholstery become one without being too much.

Above: A ceramic orchid sculpture by Diana Hall
rests serenely on a simple round stand.

Opposite: A handsome, rich brown Empire cabinet gives weight to this
corner of the room and balances out all its decorative detailing.

METFORD FRIEZE   HANDPRINTED

Opposite: Wallpaper samples make an impromptu collage.

Above: Little items can have pride of place when silhouetted on a small shelf.

———

Overleaf: Green tones soothe and a taxidermy bear surprises in a stately library.

Pages 166–67: A grand Victorian-era museum sofa
mimics the circular cast-iron staircase.

Opposite: Bookshelves are perfect stages for more than just books: alternate books with displays of collections and vignettes of diverse objects for greater depth and personality.

Above: Textural bliss: a taxidermy deer nestles on a patchwork velvet throw.

Overleaf left: A hallway densely hung with art, mirrors, maps, and taxidermy leads to a Victorian-inspired sunroom. The photomural of tropical plants on the far wall beckons you toward the room.

Overleaf right: A column of tintypes fills the narrow area between doorframes, proving that even the smallest of spaces can offer visual delight.

WUNDERKAMMER

I'm a modernist at heart, but I adore beautiful things, and I have a passion for collecting and displaying them. So how do you reconcile the two? One solution is to confine your collection within the natural boundaries of cabinets and shelves. It's like creating a miniature world and allows you to display a lot in an orderly way, as illustrated by the cabinet of curiosities on the facing page. Think natural history museum: cabinets, shelves, glass domes, and display cases. You can fill them with seashells, rock specimens, glass bottles, dolls, toys—practically any small collectibles.

Grouping objects en masse can have an impressive visual effect. Examples are . . .

- A cupboard filled with antique white ironstone dishes or an array of brightly colored midcentury glass. Remember, there is power in numbers.

- Glass-fronted cabinets are the go-to receptacles, but don't rule out cabinets with solid doors. In a way, they offer the best of both worlds: a collection can go on hiatus with ease, only to be revealed again with the opening of a door.

- Walls are also wonderful places to display a collection. Cover an entire wall with your favorite pictures, fill narrow shelf moldings and the corners of rooms with art and objects.

- Use normally unused spaces to get more of what your love out and on display.

Taking on Textures

When we think about texture, it's usually the tactile version that first comes to mind. But the concept of texture is about much more than touch. Texture is everywhere. It can be a rich layering that conjures a whole textural world. It can evoke feelings and transport you to another place, depending on how you respond to the softness of a velvet pillow or the coarseness of an old butcher block. Even purely visual texture elicits powerful reactions. Papering walls with old book pages or images from encyclopedias is one example. Enlarging vacation photos and repurposing them as wallpaper is another.

Opposite: Layered floral carpets, an embroidered canopy, and a wool blanket give this bedroom a dreamy softness. A carpetbag underneath the bed adds more texture while also serving as smart storage for extra linens.

A room provides endless surfaces to play with. Walls are a prominent place to start, but a simple tabletop or shelf, carefully curated, can have a significant impact as well. Stacking old painted-tin boxes on a coffee table is a subtle way to introduce texture. Patterns are a great way to provide an illusion of texture, and layering different patterns multiplies the effect. Playing textures off one another can be evocative as well: rough next to smooth, matte next to polished, hard next to soft. Opposites attract and can surprise and delight. The way you arrange and layer textures in your home is a physical manifestation of your personality. After all, when you invite someone to visit you, you are inviting them into your private world.

Opposite: A dressing room does double duty as a lounging area.

Below: Stacked boxes with varied painted surfaces add color and interest.

Overleaf: In an eighteenth-century tavern, the hand-stenciled walls
and ceiling create a graphic, almost modern backdrop.

Opposite: Mounting hand-painted floral murals on an ornate wallpaper is an excellent example of the aesthetic effect that layering different surfaces can have.

Above: Blues and greens weave in and out of the textures in this library. Even the bookbindings contribute to the textural mix.

———

Overleaf left: Shallow shelves hold a rotating display of pictures.

Overleaf right: Pages of old newspapers give this bathroom a textural, aged appeal and are an inexpensive way to cover walls.

WE MAKE A HOME OUT OF A HOUSE

Above and opposite: In this converted barn, exposed wood planks
provide a warm, richly textured wall surface.

Opposite: In this cozy sleeping nook, the patchwork quilt was made from men's suiting fabrics.

Right: A detailed anatomical model of a head looks on from its perch atop a dresser.

———

Overleaf and pages 190–93: A room in the Kingston Design Showhouse in Kingston, New York, was inspired by the idea of a nineteenth-century gentleman traveler whose modestly furnished room (a daybed, a table, and a reading chair) is brimming with mementos collected on his journeys, transforming it into a personal expression of a life richly lived. The window valances, made of dried berries, palm fronds, and branches by Hops Petunia Floral, are a whimsical ode to the love of botanical creations. Photomurals of distant locations, including Panama and Vizcaya, line one wall, along with a carpet for extra textural impact. Hanging a worn rug on a wall is a great way to give it a happy new use.

Opposite and above: Floral curtains picked up at a tag
sale turn a garret into a magical tented bedroom.

———————

Overleaf: By enveloping this bedroom tucked beneath the roof in a toile
de Jouy fabric, the low-ceilinged room becomes a cozy delight.

Right: A painted Odd Fellows trunk provides textural punch in a minimally decorated bedroom, demonstrating the power that one carefully chosen object can have.

Overleaf left: The cast-iron spiral stair is a sculpture in its own right and commands the space. The combination of exposed brick walls, a smooth, bright blue plastered wall, and an antique carpet is a fine example of rough and smooth textures comingling, of opposites attracting.

Overleaf right: Ornate and simple shapes are at home in a raw loft space.

Opposite: Enlarged vacation photos of favorite botanical gardens
become the setting for an exuberant sunroom. The green of
the foliage is picked up in the art and furnishings.

Above: A taxidermy macaw seems to emerge from the paper
background, heightening the tropical fantasy.

THINK
GRAPHICALLY

Tell a story with texture. Walls are waiting for a creative application.
Papering is one of the most accessible—from store-bought wallpaper to newspaper and pages of books. Virtually any kind of ephemera can be appropriated. They all create a great sense of visual texture and elicit many emotions. Once applied to the wall, their graphics create a surface too.

Layering is key. Start with the wall as a ground and build out.
Add pictures, mirrors, and three-dimensional objects like taxidermy to add more depth and interest to the storyline—texture over texture, pattern over pattern. Quilts, carpets, and any other type of weaving can be layered over decorative wall surfaces to striking effect.

- Curtains, pillows, and throws are a natural way to add texture and warmth to an interior.
- And don't forget small objects! An old, crusty stone planter will have immediate textural impact when brought indoors.
- Any item with a timeworn patina, even a tiny tabletop tin box, can give a room a jolt of tactile warmth.
- For floors, think worn rugs over worn rugs. I often start with a room-size natural rug such as sisal or seagrass, and then layer vintage carpets over it. You can cover a whole floor in a patchwork of smaller rugs for an incredible and soft textural explosion. When you incorporate patterned furnishings on top, you further expand the narrative of the room.

ACKNOWLEDGMENTS

"The essence of all beautiful art, all great art, is gratitude."

FRIEDRICH NIETZSCHE

Like so many projects, this book has been a labor of love. It was more than ten years in the making but represents a lifetime of work. In the process, I realized all the seeming coincidences that aligned for me to get to this point, and I feel very fortunate. William Abranowicz has been along from day one and is the main reason this book exists at all. Like so many projects, it had many starts and stops, many doubts to overcome. Bill was always there, cheering me on, pushing me to keep going. His beautiful photographs illustrate my ideas in a way I could not have imagined.

I want to thank Natalie Chitwood and Christian Harder for their beautiful photographs as well.

So many have helped along the way. Thank you to Andrea Codrington Lippke, whose *New York Times* article raised the ante, and Katherine Cowles, who first planted the idea of this book. To Jennifer Kabat and Paul Dinello, for helping me early on to find my voice, and to Mimi Vu, for helping clarify the direction. To Stephen Male and Jeffery Jenkins, who helped with the initial graphic design, and David Rainbird, for all the years of brilliant design help.

Special thanks to Anderson Cooper for finding the time in a hectic schedule to write such a lovely foreword.

To the Vendome Press family: Mark Magowan and Nina Magowan, for their instant and never-ending enthusiasm; Jackie Decter, for her concise editing; and Jim Spivey, for helping it all run smoothly. I am humbled to be a part of the Vendome Press library.

To Mark Melnick, for designing the book with such gorgeous rhythm and flow.

When I opened Kabinett & Kammer, I had no idea how much it would enrich my life. So many friendships have walked through the front door of the shop, and social media has given me a whole new K&K family, for which I'm deeply grateful.

To all the homeowners whose houses appear in this book, you are my most generous partners in crime.

The idea of home as a sanctuary is more relevant than ever before. To have a home that we can call our own is a privilege we cannot overestimate. I hope that this book inspires you to create and, more importantly, share not just your home but the idea of home.

Much love,

Sean

Opposite: Lilies in full bloom fill a transferware
pitcher atop an antique stone tabletop.

KABINETT & KAMMER: CREATING AUTHENTIC INTERIORS

First published in 2020 by The Vendome Press

Vendome is a registered trademark of The Vendome Press, LLC

LONDON

63 Edith Grove, London,

SW10 0LB, UK

NEW YORK

Suite 2043, 244 Fifth Avenue

New York, NY 10001

www.vendomepress.com

Distributed in North America by Abrams Books

Distributed in the United Kingdom, and the rest of the world, by Thames & Hudson

ISBN 978-0-86565-382-5

Publishers:

Beatrice Vincenzini, Mark Magowan, and Francesco Venturi

Editor: Jacqueline Decter

Production Director: Jim Spivey

Designer: Mark Melnick

Library of Congress Cataloging-in-Publication Data

Names: Scherer, Sean, 1968- author. | Abranowicz, William, photographer (expression)

Title: Sean Scherer's Kabinett & Kammer : creating authentic interiors / Sean Scherer ; foreword by Anderson Cooper ; photography by William Abranowicz.

Other titles: Kabinett & Kammer : creating authentic interiors

Description: New York : Vendome, 2020.

Identifiers: LCCN 2020021861 | ISBN 9780865653825 (hardcover)

Subjects: LCSH: Scherer, Sean, 1968---Themes, motives. | Collectibles in interior decoration--United States. | Antiques in interior decoration--United States.

Classification: LCC NK2004.3.S35 A4 2020 | DDC 747.092--dc23

LC record available at https://lccn.loc.gov/2020021861

Printed and bound in China by 1010 Printing International Ltd.

Second printing

Photo Credits

All photos by William Abranowicz, with the exception of the following: Imaginechina Limited / Alamy Stock Photo: p. 14 top; Dwight Cendrowski / Alamy Stock Photo: p. 17; Library of Congress, Prints & Photographs Division, HABS, Reproduction number HABS FLA,13-MIAM,5—77: p. 18 top; Reproduction number HABS FLA,13-MIAM,5—49: p. 18 bottom; ClassicStock / Alamy Stock Photo: p. 19; Photograph © Andy Sweet: p. 20; Danita Delimont / Alamy Stock Photo: p. 22; Library of Congress, Prints & Photographs Division, Gottscho-Schleisner Collection [LC-G613-T-67025]: p. 23 top; Photograph © Norman McGrath: p. 23 bottom; Plate 321, Roseate Spoonbill, artwork by John James Audubon: pp. 24–25; Sean Scherer: pp. 15, 16, 31, 39, 44, 45, 47, 54, 93, 184, 208; Natalie Chitwood: pp. 34, 50–51, 85, 86, 87, 138–39, 140–41, 143; Christian Harder: pp. 49, 59

Pages 2–3: A comfy blue living room is the perfect spot for reading and entertaining. When filled with family and friends, it comes to life.

Pages 4–5: A shelf of rectangular tin boxes and another featuring objects with a circular theme create a compelling still life.

Page 6: The combo of yellow and gray covering the walls and architectural trim creates a graphic background for simple, utilitarian, white-painted furniture and a collection of mid-century ceramics.